Wreck & F

round the Cornish coast

Richard & Bridget Larn

For further information of all the titles in this series please visit:-
www.tormark.co.uk

First published 2006
Reprinted 2007

Published by Tor Mark, United Downs Ind Est, Redruth,
Cornwall TR16 5HY

Copyright Richard & Bridget Larn @ 2006

Designed by Alix Wood, www.alixwood.co.uk

Printed by R Booth Ltd
Antron Hill, Mabe, Penryn TR10 9HH

ISBN **978 085025 406 8**

Front Cover: Sennen lifeboat *Four Boys* - Mersey class in service Dec 1991 to Dec 1998 (RNLI)

Title Page: Coxswain David Grubb, Padstow lifeboat 1899-1900. He was to lose his life in the loss of two lifeboats on the 11th April 1900; also drowned was his only son James whom he took reluctantly as a deck hand when they were undermanned. (*The Story of Padstow's Lifeboats*, Claude Berry, 1977, Lodeneck Press)

Inside Front & Back Covers: The *Sauveterre* July 2005 (MOD)

Back Cover: Rescue by breeches-buoy from the *City of Cardiff* Nanjizal Bay Land's End 21 March 1912 - 25 crew & passengers saved (John Behenna)

Before Lifeboats

THE EARLIEST REFERENCE to a shipwreck in the British Isles dates back to the beginning of the 12th century, and for at least the next 400 years there was little regard by the Crown, local authorities or ordinary people for a shipwreck other than its value; what did it carry and what of the cargo could they steal? Ships of the period were seldom identified by name, only by their owners, an example being a wreck of February 1282, 'belonging to Henry Flik and Helenbrand de Lubek, merchants of Alman'. There was seldom regard for the legal owners of a ship driven ashore, nor its crew, and the 'rude country people', more commonly called 'wreckers', would descend on a ship literally in their thousands, abandoning their work and homes, making their way to the coast from many miles inland in order to loot a ship. In a 19th century incident when the French *Le Landois* went ashore in a cove near Cape Cornwall in 1837, 25 Coastguards faced a drunken mob of over 4,000 men, women and children, and the the Rev Buller of St Just was called on to read the Riot Act. People became so drunk on stolen wine and cordials, they were arrested and carried off to gaol unconscious.

A Wrecking at Godrevy

On Thursday morning last, during a snow fall and a strong N gale, the brig *Mary* drove ashore at Fassel Geaver Cove. Driving over the rocks she went on the beach and the crew were saved. Men were hired to work on the ship securing her stores, and keep watch at night on what had been saved. Next day Camborne miners came down, cutting the ship's cables, carried off her two smallest anchors, stole all the beef and biscuits, and even had the hardihood before it became dark, to steal the seamen's clothing at Gwithian Churchtown which had been washed by the people for the poor fellows, and hung up to dry. In their pillage they set the watch at defiance by threatening to cut them down with dags and hatchets. The vessel and cargo belong to the Captain, who is not insured, now ruined and destitute. The wreckers are identified, apprehended, and committed for trial at the Assize.

West Briton 28 March 1817

The only sea law in those early days was the *Rolls of Oleron*, or *Judgements d'Oleron*, whose roots were in even earlier Rhodian law, which came to Europe from the Mediterranean with the Romans, to be adopted successively by France, England and later Spain. Our adoption of the *Rolls of Oleron* recognised the injustice of 'wrecking' as well as the so-called 'Right of Wreck', a peculiarity of English law steeped in history. Originally granted to a lord or wealthy landowner by the Crown who, having no standing army or navy to fight their wars for them, gave this right in lieu of payment for providing armed men, horses or ships during a conflict. It meant that the benefactor had legal entitlement to any wrecked ships or goods on his land in perpetuity, despite the fact that the Crown was actually giving away ownership of items that were not theirs to give away in the first place!

The law had a two-fold purpose, to exact punishment on a pilot who might be tempted to deliberately run a ship ashore for plunder, and to recognize the rights of both ship owners and those owning cargo. Regarding the pilots, the law stated:

If any pilot deliberately misguides a shyp that it may be cast away, he shall be put to a rigorous death and hang in chayns; and if the Lord of the place where a shyp be thus lost abet such villans in order to have a share of the wreck, his person shall be fastyned to a stake in the midst of his own mansion, which, being fired at the four corners, shall be burnt to the ground and he with it.

As to the rights of ownership of ships, their cargo and crews:

A shyp.... on entering into a haven or elsewhere, by chaunce breaketh yp and perysseth, and the mayster, mariners and merchaunts dye, theyr goodes are cast on the coast or remayne in the sea without any pursyte on the parte of those to whome they belonge, for they know nothynge in siche a case, the whiche is very piteouse, the Lord ought to set persons to save the sayd goodes, and these goodes the Lord ought to guard and place safely and afterwards he ought to make known to the relatives or relations of the dead drowned the misfortune and paye the sayd salvors after their labour and payne that they have taken, not at his expense but at the expense of the thynges saved, and the resedue the which remayneth, the Lord ought to guard or have guarded entirely till a yere, unless those to whom the sayd goodes belonge come sooner. At the ende of a yere passed or more, if it pleaseth the sayd Lord to wayte, he ought to sell publically and to the highest offerer the sayd things, and from the money receved he ought to have prayer made to God for the dead, or to marrye poor maydes, or do other workes after reason and conscience. And he who shall do the contrarie and shall take any of the goodes of the sayd poor persons shipwrecked, lost and drowned against theyr desire and wyll, he is excommunicated from the church. This is the judgment.

Between 1340 and 1357 the first Admiralty Courts in England sat to deal with enforcement of maritime law, and two retired admirals, were appointed, one for the 'north' the other for the 'south & west', and later every coastal county had a vice-admiral who was supposed to administer justice and uphold the law of wreck and salvage. They were required to collect the Crown's

▼ *Coastguard rescue team at Mawgan Porth – possibly after the successful rescue of the crew of the* Seine *27 December 1900.*

(Tony Pawlyn)

share of the spoils, but generally grew rich on the proceeds of wrecks of which the Crown were never informed, particularly in remote Cornwall or the even more remote Isles of Scilly. The result was a farce, since there were no standard maps or charts, so that the coastal limits or boundaries of a particular manor house and hence its 'Right of Wreck' was constantly in dispute. Floating wreckage and cargo known as flotsam, was frequently found at sea and towed in by boatmen, which led to another dispute, how far offshore did the 'Right of Wreck' extend? The definitions were as many and varied as the vice-admirals themselves: 'as far out to sea as umber barrel can be seen'; 'as far as an arrow can be shot'; ' as far out to sea as a man mounted on a horse can stick a spear in the bottom', and even more ambiguous, 'as far as a cannon shot', none of which were a definite or even measurable distance. There was even a time when the law stated that 'a ship is not a wreck provided a man, cat or dog escapes from it alive' What greater incentive could there be to commit murder, or leave a sailor to die on the foreshore?

It was very much a case of 'the Lord giveth and the Lord taketh away'. Of course it was not morally right to steal wreck goods or strip a body of its shoes, but if you had nothing and were barefoot, as the old saying went, 'the dead have no use for clothes'. Most wrecks were strandings and easy to get at, being lost in shallow water, simply because wooden vessels tended to stay afloat if they were holed or capsized, sinking in deep water only when far from land. If rescue of survivors was considered, from offshore rocks for example, then local boatmen might put to sea but only after they had first secured their share of wreck goods. Occasionally, a wealthy gentleman or squire, a less callous ignorer of calamity, might offer boatmen monetary incentives to rescue people, and such benefactors frequently accompanied the rescuers to sea in their small craft to give encouragement.

The first Life - Saving boats

BECAUSE OF BRITAIN'S long maritime history there has been a general misconception that this country was among the first to have craft stationed on the coast dedicated to life-saving. Whilst the true birth place of a water rescue service started in China 300 years ago, it would nevertheless be true to say that Britain not only developed seagoing lifeboats, but also established the first truly national lifeboat organization around its coastline. Trade and transport within the Chinese interior was almost totally dependent on waterborne traffic on its many canals, waterways and rivers, each with a myriad of natural hazards. Travellers and traders alike had to run the gauntlet of rapids, rock strewn gorges and sandbanks and were no doubt grateful for the many life-saving societies set up on the banks of rivers like the Yangtze. The speedy recovery of bodies from upset or stranded vessels had a greater religious significance in China than in the west, since the Chinese greatly revere their ancestors and it is of enormous importance that a family knows exactly where their loved ones are buried. To lose someone by drowning and then not have a body to bury was considered both an enormous tragedy and a stigma on the relatives.

The *Chinkiang Association for Saving Life* was set up by wealthy benefactors near Nanking on the lower levels of the Yangtze River around 1708. On the upper reaches of that river it is recorded that five lifeboats were established in 1737 by order of the

First Duchy Lifeboat Station

Whereas several Wrecks happened last winter in the Mount's Bay, and many lives were unfortunately lost; on representation of which to the Committee at Lloyd's, they have liberally contributed the sum of FIFTY Pounds, towards the purchase of a Life-boat for the said Bay, the full cost of which will be about ONE HUNDRED & FIFTY POUNDS. The inhabitants thereof, and of Cornwall in general are requested to contribute towards carrying this laudable undertaking into effect; for which purpose subscriptions are received at the Penzance, Falmouth and Helston Banks, and at the Cornish Bank, Truro.

Royal Cornwall Gazette
29 October 1803

Emperor, but there are no surviving records in the archives of the Imperial Chinese Maritime Customs to tell us who manned them or how successful they were. Knowledge of what the Chinese were doing regarding life-saving almost certainly reached Europe via the commercial activities of the various East India Companies, and in Britain through the Honourable English East India Company during the 17th and 18th centuries. This led to the formation in Amsterdam in

1767 of an *Institution for the Recovery of Drowned Persons,* and by 1773 similar schemes were introduced in Paris, Hamburg, Padua, Venice and Milan.

In Britain the *Humane Society for the Recovery of Persons Appararently Drowned* was started in 1774, and soon similar societies existed all round the coast.That at Liverpool offered a guinea for every life saved, and half a guinea for an unsuccessful attempt when a body showed no sign of life after being pulled from the sea. Local minds were naturally focused on the catastrophe of 1764, when 18 ships stranded at the entrance to the Mersey in one night, drowning over 75 people.

The first lifeboat station established in Britain was at Formby in 1776, and the minutes of the Liverpool Common Council of 2 April that year read:

> *Richard Scarisbrick of Formby, sailor, be appointed to take care of the Boat and Boat House erected and provided to be built and stationed at Formby to assist and save shipwrecked persons and goods on this Coast . . . he and the Boat's crew shall be handsomely rewarded hereafter for such good service done herein and not less than one Guinea per head for every Life or person they shall save.*

Saving the Crew of the *Suffolk*

Tuesday last, in a violent Gale of wind at NE, the ship *Suffolk* of London, six months out from Bengal with bale goods and rice, arrived in St. Ives Bay with all her sails split, leaking and the water level rising. Of her 21 crew only 6 were able to do duty, the remainder being sick. By the vigilant exertions of the people on Shore (who always in such cases distinguish themselves by manly alacrity), got boats from the creek at Hayle, and even carried a large eight-oared boat 3 miles overland from St. Ives, and attempted at all hazards to get to the ship. Her Captain and crew floated a keg attached to a line to the boat, which was taken ashore and by this means hauled all the people on shore one by one, except two who were so ill were unable to struggle and so died in their hammocks.

Royal Cornwall Gazette & Sherborne Mercury, 6 March 1802

It is worth noting that in 1825, on the foundation of the *National Institution for the Preservation of Life from Shipwreck*, forerunner to the RNLI (Royal National Lifeboat Institution), the little station at Formby had been in existence for 50 years.

The initiative to develop a 'un-sinkable' lifeboat in Britain came from the Newcastle area, brought about by the wreck of a collier, the **Adventure**, on 15 March 1789, when the greater part of her crew perished only 300 yards from shore, in front of hundreds of spectators. A reward of two guineas was offered for the best design, which was won by a South Shields boat builder, Henry Greathead, who named his trial boat of this type **Original**, which made its first rescue on 30 January 1790. Some historians have claimed Bamburgh Castle as the nation's first true lifeboat station, but this has naturally been disputed, bearing in mind the early developments at Liverpool. By 1810 some 44 lifeboats had been built by Henry Greathead and sold throughout Europe, and his name soon became synonymous with this type of craft.

▲ *Stranded so close to the shore there was hardly room to launch the Penzance lifeboat* Dora *(1884-1895), to the French brigantine* Jeune Hortense, *bound for Poole in ballast, which drove ashore on 17 May 1888 at Longrock, Eastern Green. Her three man crew and a boy were rescued, watched by a large crowd of bystanders.* (Gibsons of Scilly)

The first West Country lifeboats

BY COINCIDENCE THE West Country received its first three lifeboats, all built by Greathead, in the same year. Philip Langmead, MP for the borough of Plymouth and a former Mayor, donated a Greathead lifeboat to the port, the first in the south-west, which arrived in Sutton-Pool on 20 July 1803, but its fame was short lived. From 1803 until 1825 there is not a single mention of Plymouth's lifeboat being used in any records or newspaper accounts, and it must be assumed this boat either decayed or was withdrawn through disuse.

Neither is there any record of what happened to the first Exmouth lifeboat stationed there sometime in 1803; this 30ft boat was paid for by £50 from the Corporation of Lloyd's, the balance of a further £100 coming from local subscribers. It was 1858 before Exmouth had another lifeboat, named **Victoria**, by which time the whole lifeboat organisation around the country was under the auspices of the RNLI.

On 21 October 1803, Penzance also received a 27ft double-ended Greathead lifeboat, which rowed ten oars, built with a grant from Lloyd's and a further £100 collected locally. Like the Plymouth boat, which went

Plymouth's First Lifeboat

Yesterday afternoon a good procession of boats, decorated with colours, streamers etc, rowed and sailed to Hamoaze to visit and conduct the Life Boat to Plymouth. It was received at the entrance of the harbour with a band of music, playing 'God Save the King' and was rowed, the rowers dressed in whiteshirts, black velvet caps, decorated with blue ribands, by ten seamen. As the boat passed the shipping, it was saluted and also received a royal salute from Mr T. Lockyer's Battery, Teat's Hill, of 21 guns. The Mayor, accompanied by the principal merchants and local inhabitants, proceeded to the Prince George Tavern, and partook of a very elegant cold collation and dessert of Fruit, wines etc. and the evening concluded with the greatest festivity.

Felix Farley's Bristol Journal,
21 July 1803

The Wreck of the *Harmonia*

The two opposite qualities of rapine and humanitarianism were displayed at Portreath on 4th November when the Portuguese brigantine *Harmonia,* Oporto to Sligo with wine, oranges and cork, drove ashore in a severe storm. Captain Bidder, whose vessel lay inside Portreath Quay, put out in a boat with five local men to rescue those on board. In the violence of the surf the frail craft upset, and three would-be rescuers drowned. Captain Bidder and two men were cast ashore in a senseless condition. A subsequent rescue saved the captain and eight crew. Others, of a more mercenary inclination, were making preparations to plunder the cargo. Informed of the ugly situation Lord de Dunstanville and Colonel Lemon, with a company of Artillery, went to Portreath to prevent the wreck becoming the prey of the local populace. John Crowthers, one of the drowned rescuers leaves a widow and seven small children, only one old enough to earn a living. The harsh terms of Parish Relief means she gets no help unless she returns to Tewkesbury, her husband's home town. A Public Subscription was launched and a considerable sum raised to succour this unfortunate man's dependants.'

Cornishman, 9 November 1807

unused except for practice for 22 years, the Penzance lifeboat performed not one service in nine years, and in fact was offered for sale on 1 July 1812 'in distress for rent', going for just 20 guineas, since the town's corporation could no longer pay the rent of the boathouse.

By 1824 influential men in London, led by Sir William Hillary of the Isle of Man, had formed the *Royal National Institution for the Preservation of Life from Shipwreck* , and the number of lifeboats around the coast was greatly increased. There were of course many who opposed the idea of men risking their lives in lifeboats, arguing that it was better to rescue survivors from the shore, by throwing lines across a wreck, which made sense if a vessel ended up stranded in the shallows, the surf zone, or against high cliffs where they would be inaccessible from seaward anyway. Early experiments with line-throwing apparatus were conducted at Woolwich Arsenal in August 1791, when a Sergeant Bell of the Royal Artillery tested a mortar, firing a shell carrying a heavy 'deep-sea' line over 1,200ft. Bell received a reward of 50 guineas and was promoted from Sergeant to Lieutenant, but died shortly after, his idea never being developed.

By a remarkable coincidence, two men at opposite ends of the country, Henry Trengrouse of Helston, Cornwall, and Captain George Manby, barracks' master of an artillery depot at Gt Yarmouth, Norfolk, witnessed two different shipwrecks in 1807 which had a profound effect on them. Both spent the rest of their lives developing means of passing communicating lines to vessels in distress. Manby saw the crew of HM gun-brig **Snipe** drown only 50 yards offshore at Yarmouth on 18 February, whilst Trengrouse watched with horror as over 100 men were lost from HM Frigate **Anson**, 100 yards off Loe Bar, near his home town that December. Manby's military background naturally caused him to pursue what he called his 'wreck-gun', and by 1814 with virtually free access to army stores and manpower, around 45 Manby mortars were in use around the country. Its inventor received a huge reward of £2,000

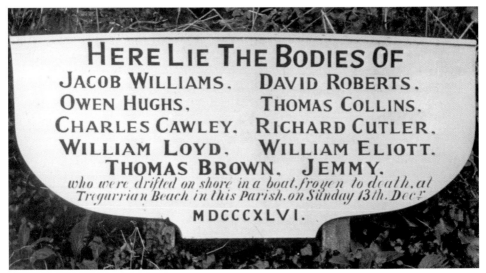

▲ *A replica of a longboat transom, the original having long since rotted and fallen apart, which was erected in 1866 as a memorial in Mawgan churchard, to ten men who were found frozen to death in a boat driven ashore at Tregurrian beach on 13 December that year. They had been aboard the Liverpool barque* Hope, *which had been abandoned off the Welsh coast as she started to sink. (Clive Carter)*

and was made an honorary member of the *Royal Humane Society*, the device later being purchased by other countries, including the USA.

In contrast Henry Trengrouse developed his rocket life-saving apparatus entirely at his own expense, receiving very little financial help or public acclaim. Its cheapness and portability eventually caused it to be adopted by both the Board of Trade and the Coastguard Service, and known generally as the 'breeches-buoy' apparatus, survived in service around the entire United Kingdom coastline until the late 1980s, by which time a helicopter rescue service had been established. That Henry Trengrouse and the potential of his invention were still not fully appreciated is reflected in an article in the *Penzance Journal* of 30 June 1847:

Loss of His Majesty's brig *Snipe*

The dreadful events of the 18th February, 1807, when His Majesty's gun-brig *Snipe* was driven on shore near Haven's Mouth at Yarmouth, first made an impression upon my mind, which has never been effaced. At the close of that melancholy scene, after several hours of fruitless attempts to save the crew, upwards of 60 persons were lost, though not more than fifty yards from shore, and this wholly owing to the impossibility of conveying a rope to their assistance. At that crisis a ray of hope beamed upon me, and I resolved immediately to devote my mind to the discovery of some means for affording relief in cases of similar distress and difficulty.

George Manby. 'An Essay on the Preservation of Shipwrecked Persons' given to the R S A October 1808

Reward of Merit. Mr Trengrouse of Helston, who has so nobly and disinterestedly exerted himself on behalf of sailors, has just obtained from the National Shipwreck Institution the sum of five sovereigns to be distributed among the brave men, who at the risk of their lives, rescued the master and three of the crew of the late schooner **Elizabeth,** *of Bergen, wrecked at Gunwalloe on 20 November last.*

Note that the 'brave men' got five sovereigns between them, whilst Henry Trengrouse received nothing! If comparisons are made between the two inventions, Manby's apparatus was heavy and cumbersome, and the rapid acceleration of the ball

The Wreck of
HM. Frigate *Anson*

The **Anson** drove in amongst the breakers which were crashing with great fury on Loe Bar. The tremendous sea broke over the ship's masts, which soon went by the board, the mainmast forming a kind of floating bridge to the shore, along which many of the crew were able to escape. Captain Lydiard, RN, who behaved with great gallantry on this occasion, lost his life when endeavouring to extricate a boy entangled below the mast, being three times washed away by heavy seas, the last of which swept him to his death. Estimates of the number lost vary from 60 to 100. The captain was buried at Falmouth, other victims being bundled in heaps into large pits dug in the cliff above, without any burial rites, this being the customary practice at the time.

C. Noall & G. Farr, Vol.2, 'Wreck and Rescue round the Cornish Coast'

from the barrel frequently caused the line it carried to break, whilst the track of the projectile could not be seen at night. In contrast, Trengrouse's apparatus was light-weight, its rockets accelerated gradually so seldom if ever broke the line, and their trail of smoke and fire allowed both those ashore and afloat to follow its track, which greatly assisted aiming in strong wind conditions and at night. However, powder - filled rockets were often unstable, and being subject to damp became unreliable in storage, and it took improvements by John Dennet in 1832 and Colonel Boxer in the 1860s, to produce a reliable rocket with a consistent range of at least 400 yards. Between 1870 and 1911 some 10,000 lives were saved from shipwrecks using rockets and breeches-buoys.

His line carrying rocket could be fired from a standard musket, making the apparatus cheap, light, portable and eminently simple. He laboured to perfect it for 10 years, gambling some £3,000 on his invention, then asked the Admiralty to carry out tests. They in turn gave orders in 1818 that copies of the original should be placed in every dockyard, to enable naval officers to familiarize themselves with its use; Trinity House even recommended that no ship should be without one. Despite an initial order for 20 sets, manufacture was then taken over by the Admiralty, and Trengrouse received only £50 from the navy, with 30 guineas and a silver medal from the Society of Arts. The Tsar of Russia was so taken by the invention that he sent Trengrouse a letter and a valuable diamond ring, which he was forced to pawn and later sell in order to support his wife, ten children and his home at 122 Meneage Street, Helston.

The next West Country lifeboat was the *Mariner's Friend*, built to order at Padstow by John Tredwen in 1827, costing £50, she was only 23ft long and rowed four oars. She is believed to have been kept at the quay until 1829, when a permanent lifeboat station was built by the *Padstow Harbour Association for the Preservation of Life and Property from Shipwreck,* at Hawker's Cove, nearer to Stepper Point, the much feared Doom Bar, and the open sea. The north coast of Cornwall and Devon is entirely devoid of any sheltered deep-water anchorage and the small ports of St Ives, Newquay, Padstow, Boscastle and Bude, all of which are tidal, offer limited refuge for only small vessels. Consequently it is

Henry Trengrouse, of Helston

Among those hundreds of spectators who flocked to the wreck of the *Anson*, was a young man from Helston, Henry Trengrouse. Deeply moved by the scenes he had witnessed, he gave much thought to the problem of how to bring help to shipwrecked seamen by establishing some communication from the shore. He devised a form of rocket apparatus for carrying a line to a ship, this invention being far safer and less cumbersome than the shot & chain proposed by Lieut Bell in 1791, and Captain Manby's mortar which was exhibited in 1807. Trengrouse devoted his life and sacrificed his fortune perfecting his apparatus, endeavouring to win Government support which never came and he died in poverty in 1854. He also invented the cork lifejacket, and his rockets or 'travellers' as he called them, were later taken up by the Board of Trade to become the 'breeches-buoy' apparatus.

Royal Cornwall Gazette,
December 1854

notorious for shipwrecks, but it still took until the 1850s before there was any degree of lifeboat coverage for the area. Bude took delivery of its first lifeboat in 1837, the direct outcome of two shipwrecks on the same day, 29 October 1836. Although based on the original Greathead design, it was a 'North Country' surf boat designed for rowing only eight oars, and like other lifeboats built outside of the West Country did not find favour with Cornish boatmen, who felt them unsuitable for local conditions. It only ever made one service launch, which was in October 1843, with a near disaster the following year when it capsized during practice.

By the mid 1840s there were still only twelve lifeboat stations throughout Devon and Cornwall, with little hope of any further additions, but the election of a new President of the Shipwreck Institution in 1851, the 4th Duke of Northumberland, who had the support of both Queen Victoria and Prince Albert, brought about a revival in the public's awareness of lifeboats and wrecks. The institution created the new post of inspector of lifeboats, who organized training and visited all the stations, and for the first time, lifeboat men were paid on going afloat, regardless of whether on service or practice. At the same time lifeboat coxswains received an annual salary, in addition to 'afloat' money. Within four years other changes included transferral of all 'line-throwing' equipment to the coastguards, still manned by Royal Navy Reservists; the care of shipwreck survivors was handed to the *Shipwrecked Fishermen & Mariners Royal Benevolent Society*, and the name of the overall organization changed to the *Royal National Life-boat Institution*.

To assist the newly formed organization, the government's *Mercantile Marine Fund* made an annual grant of £2,000, until such time as voluntary fund-raising could make the Institution self-sufficient. This was achieved by 1860, and the RNLI to this day is still supported solely by public contributions.

Lifeboat accidents in Cornwall

Bude – 1844

A lifeboat was presented by the Duchy of Cornwall to Bude under banner headlines in *Felix Farley's Bristol Journal* which read, *Royal Munificence & Humanity*. The newspaper went on to say:

> *During the late storm two shipwrecks occurred off the village of Bude. We have authority to state, that when the circumstance was represented to the King, and that*

no means were provided even for endeavouring to save the lives of his subjects in such extreme peril on the coast, so remarkable for shipwrecks, His Majesty most promptly and munificently commanded that a sum of money should be given for the purpose of establishing a life-boat at Bude.

The lifeboat was delivered in 1837, but unusually, was never named. She launched on exercise on 10 October 1844, and was off the harbour when a surge broke first the steering oar, then four others on the port side, and she slewed round beam-on, so that the next wave caused her to capsize. Five men were trapped beneath the hull until she drifted into shallow water when they escaped, a fifth climbed on top of the hull, two clung to oars until saved, but a William Skitch and Nicholas Bradden drowned.

Padstow – 1867

Three lifeboats at Padstow had saved 57 lives between them over a period of 40 years without incident until 1867, when the **Albert Edward**, built by Forrest's of Limehouse, on the Thames, bought for £224 by the City of Bristol Fund, was driven ashore on the St Minver coast, in the Camel Estuary. The lifeboat ended up ashore on the beach with hardly a scratch on it, but five men, three of them coastguards, lost their lives, without even reaching the wreck they went out to assist. The vessel in distress was the schooner **Georgiana**, of Boston, Lincs, Rouen to Cork carrying plaster of Paris. She had rounded Stepper Point and was in sheltered water when the ebb tide caught her, and despite dropping two anchors, both of which dragged, she went ashore on the much feared Doom Bar, from which hardly any vessels ever escaped. Maroons brought the lifeboat crew together, from both Hawker's Cove where the boat was housed, and nearby Padstow, and she was launched under oars. Unusually, the chief coastguard officer, Daniel Shea was on board, along with two of his boatmen and others, backing up Coxswain William Hill's crew of seven men, making 13 in total.

Four oars were broken in attempting to close on the wreck in heavy seas, so they drove over Doom Bar, making for Polzeath Cove. Suddenly, waves causing her to fill, more oars were broken, and seconds later she capsized, end over end. All but two of her crew were thrown out, then she capsized again, only this time she did not right herself for some five minutes, leaving all 13 men struggling in a cold wintry sea.

▲ *The German steel schooner* Adolf Vinnen *was only nine days out of her builder's yard, when she was driven ashore by a gale on 23 February 1923. She struck a little to the west of Bass Point, near the Lizard at 5.30pm. All the crew were saved by breeches-buoy from the cliff top. (Richard Larn Collection)*

Spectators scrambled down Trebetherick cliffs to assist, throwing ropes to the struggling figures, and helping them ashore. Of the five who lost their lives, including the chief coastguard officer, three were never found. As for the wreck, it lifted off Doom Bar on the tide by itself, drifted ashore and went to pieces; only one of her crew being lost.

Bude Haven – 1877

Bude Haven, which had been given its first lifeboat funded by King William IV in 1837, was into its fourth boat without any serious incidents when, on 3 March 1877, disaster struck. A locally owned sailing barge, the **Elizabeth Scown**, went down the coast to collect a cargo of granite

▲ *Five members of the crew of the Dieppe trawler* Jeanne Gougy
*had a remarkable escape on 3 November 1962. The vessel drove
ashore at 5am, on the northern side of Dr Syntax's Head at
Land's End and shortly after fell over on its port side, trapping
four men and a boy completely underwater in her wheelhouse.
Somehow they managed to survive in an air pocket until the
next low water at 11am, when one of them, waving an arm
through a window, was seen by a woman on the cliff top. (Clive
Carter)*

Fearful Disaster on the Cornish Coast

Loss of Steamer and 11 lives

The Cornish coast off Portreath was the scene of a fearful disaster on Friday....rockets were fired and a tar barrel was ignited on the cliffs ....the Hayle lifeboat which had in the meantime arrived via Camborne had been backed onto the edge of the sea, but the carriage sunk in the deep sand and the efforts to move her proved fruitless for a few moments....a glance showed two men endeavouring by the help of lifebelts and spars to swim to the land....a rush again was made for the lifeboat and the crew once more took up their positions while a still more energetic effort was made to launch her. This effort proved more successful and amid cheers the 'E F Harrison' floated off, and soon got on top of the breakers.

West Briton 31 January 1895

for use in the enlargement of Bude church. At night she struck the reef at the back of the breakwater, and became stranded. Whilst the lifeboat was being launched, the coastguards fired a rocket line across her, bringing the ship's boy ashore. A journalist watched as the lifeboat attempted to get close to the wreck in enormous seas, describing the event later as 'an act of almost insane heroism'. Unable to get close to the wreck, the lifeboat turned back for the harbour, then a tremendous wave struck, destroying her rudder and breaking several oars, leaving it quite unmanageable. Hit by a second huge wave the lifeboat capsized, throwing all 12 crew into the sea. As the boat righted itself, eleven men managed to drag themselves over the gunwhales and back into the lifeboat, or else struggled through the surf to reach the shore. All eleven owed their lives to the regulation cork lifejackets they were wearing, the missing coxswain, James Maynard, being the only man not to have put one on. Some say his body was never found, other sources say it was found days after, totally mangled and unidentifiable, apart from his clothing.

Hayle – 1882

During a gale on 16 November 1882, the schooner *Susan Elizabeth* was seen under Black Cliffs in distress, her crew assembled in the bow, trying to keep above the waves. The lifeboat *Isis,* which had been on station since 1866 put out, watched by hundreds of spectators overlooking the wreck site. It took half-an-hour to row the lifeboat to windward, and after anchoring she veered down on the schooner, and was alongside when the *Isis* capsized. Five of the crew were thrown clear, four others clung to her grab lines, whilst four more were trapped under the boat, but amazingly no lives were lost and the lifeboat was recovered virtually undamaged.

Hayle – 1895

Portreath had no lifeboat when the SS *Escurial* went ashore on 25 January 1895. The nearest was at Hayle, and the 34ft *New Oriental Bank* was dragged over 11 miles on her carriage, through the town of Camborne, and launched across Portreath's soft sandy beach. A gale was blowing which struck the boat in the surf zone before it was even afloat, throwing it back up the beach parallel with the shore. Those watching the scene were horrified. Offshore, a large steamer was sinking with several of its crew in the water, others clinging to the rigging or her floating mainmast which had broken off, whilst an abandoned lifeboat from the vessel lay in the shallows and eleven drowned men had already been washed ashore from the wreck.

Padstow – 1900

There is probably no other lifeboat station in the whole of the British Isles which lost two lifeboats during the same night.

On 24 October 1882, the Ramsgate lifeboat towed by the tug *Aid*, saved the crew of the yacht *Arab*, indirectly providing Padstow with two new lifeboats. The yacht had run aground on the South Goodwin Sands in a gale and her owner, a barrister named R A B Preston, grateful that he and eight friends were saved, offered £1,000 towards a new lifeboat station anywhere in the country. The money not only provided Padstow with a new lifeboat named appropriately *Arab*, but also a new lifeboat house in Trethillick Lane. Built in London, the new boat was put through acceptance trials, including capsize, on the Serpentine in London, as part of an International Fisheries Exhibition, then transported, along with her launching carriage to Truro by rail, then horse drawn by road to Hawker's Cove. From here she launched 17 times on service, saving 75 lives before she met with disaster in 1900.

With the harbour of Padstow tidal and a mile and a half upstream from Stepper Point and the open sea, there was really no merit in stationing a lifeboat at the port itself, since both the Town Bar and Doom Bar sandbanks denied vessels entry or exit at low tide. Having said that, the first Padstow lifeboat, named *Mariner's Friend*, of 1827, is believed to have been kept on the quay there but only for two years, after which a permanent lifeboat house was built at Hawker's Slip Cove, only half a mile from Stepper Point. Three boats served here before the first of two successive craft named *Arab* arrived on station.

By now the RNLI had completed experiments with steam-driven lifeboats, and with the activities of both neighbouring Port Isaac and Newquay boats, as well as the *Arab* somewhat restricted, since they were all rowing boats, the Padstow station was allocated an additional lifeboat, the new 56ft, 31-ton *James Stevens No.4*, which was kept permanently afloat on moorings out from Hawker's Cove. She arrived on station in February 1899, where she was allocated a crew of eleven, two of whom were firemen and two engineers, to look after her compound steam engine and its small, single, water-tube boiler.

The lead up to the loss of both lifeboats began with the sighting of the Lowestoft fishing ketch *Peace & Plenty* on the rocks off Greenaway within the estuary, on 11 April 1900, between Treberthick Point and Pentireglaze, surrounded by a mass of white water. In answer to rockets fired by the pilot boat, which had already attempted to reach the wreck, the *Arab* was launched into a terrible sea, totally unaware that the Trebetherick rocket brigade had already fired a line across the wreck and saved four of her eight man crew. Rowing back and forth along the coast in a roaring gale and heavy seas, unable to see the wreck, they turned back for the shelter of Stepper Point, but by now her crew were physically exhausted. The boat was suddenly hit by a huge sea which broke or carried away nine of her ten rowing oars, leaving her virtually at the mercy of the storm. Coxswain Brown ordered her anchor thrown overboard and a blue flare was burnt, indicating distress. The crew managed to get out the three spare oars and after a rest, rowed for the shore, leaving the sea to drive her on the rocks, where all 13 lifeboat men scrambled to safety, but the *Arab* was so badly damaged she was declared a total loss.

Coxswain Grubb, on the steam lifeboat, whose crew were already on stand-by, thought the distress flare came from the ketch, and on putting out steered around the west end of the Doom Bar, which the boat's draught prevented them from crossing directly. She was only minutes into her rescue mission when one enormous sea, described in a newspaper account as being 'at least 30ft high', caught her port quarter, lifting her stern completely out of the water causing her to fall beam on to the wave, and she immediately rolled over. All seven men in the cockpit were thrown into the sea, but the men in her engine-room were trapped. Closed up inside the compartment by a sealed watertight hatch and now inverted, they were scalded by boiling water,

▲ *The St Mary's lifeboat* Henry Dundas (IV), *attending the sinking full-rigged ship* Ardencraig *in Broad Sound, 8 January 1911. The last of the St Mary's rowing lifeboats before the motorised* Elsie *was introduced in 1919, this photograph shows a total of 15 men aboard a boat normally manned by just 12, not all of whom are wearing lifejackets.*
(Gibsons of Scilly)

This sequence of four photographs by Percy Holman depicts a controlled practice launch of the Penzance lifeboat Elizabeth & Blanche on a pleasant sunny afternoon about 1905; obviously in much easier conditions than would occur in an emergency. She was the second lifeboat of that name to be stationed at Penzance. She served the RNLI well being firstly at Penzance from 1899-1908; Newlyn 1908-13 and lastly at Penlee until 1922 – twenty-three years service!

(Tony Pawlyn)

▲ Helpers and crew man the 'check lines' to ensure that the five ton lifeboat doesn't run away from them on the slipway. The lifeboat house was at the bottom of Jenning's Street and therefore at high tide the boat had to manoeuvred only a few yards. At low water the lifeboat had to be dragged across the mud by a team of eight to ten horses almost to the harbour entrance.

▼ On the bit of shingle at the bottom of Jenning's Slip the helpers and crew prepare all the gear for the launch into the Abbey Basin. Propelled by twelve oars she required a crew of 15 to man her.

The crew are still sorting themselves out as the helpers push the carriage into the water. On the order 'launch' the locking pins are knocked out and the shore helpers run away with the launching falls which catapult the lifeboat forwards on her carriage. When the boat is about halfway off her carriage the whole fore-assembly tips forward launching the lifeboat dramatically into the sea.

Unfortunately this was all too fast for the cameras of the period.

▼ Moments later having cleared the arches carrying Wharf Road across the Abbey Basin the crew of the Elizabeth & Blanche manfully pull for the harbour mouth. Still riding high as she has not yet taken on her water ballast some of the crew are struggling to avoid 'catching a crab'. In a freshening breeze Coxswain Trewhella nonchalantly holds onto his hat.

Note, the rudder has been raised to avoid damage and most of the crew are still wearing the old style cork life-jackets.

The Penlee *lifeboat* Solomon Browne, *being launched from its station slipway at Penlee Point, Mousehole – a picture taken just two weeks before the disaster. (RNLI)*

mutilated and suffocated within their metal 'box', and all four men died a dreadful and very painful death. Eight locals lost their lives that night, leaving four widows and fourteen orphans.

The **Arab** was replaced by a slightly larger rowing lifeboat by the same name almost immediately and the **James Stevens** by the smaller rowing boat **Edmund Harvey**, but hard lessons had been learned at Padstow and other stations concerning steam powered lifeboats. Instead, in addition to two new lifeboats, Padstow was given a steam tug, the **Helen Peele**, a 95ft, 133-ton propeller driven vessel, to tow them to the scene of future rescues, rather than rely on sheer manpower pulling on oars.

Newquay – 1908 & 1917

The rowing lifeboat **James Stevens No.5**, built at Mevagissey, and presented to Newquay town in 1899, had saved 26 lives when she capsized during a practice launch with one crewman drowned. On 6 March 1908, a day scheduled for a lifeboat exercise, it was unfortunately blowing a strong gale, but conditions were not considered such that the exercise should be cancelled. She went out four miles, rowed and sailed around then turned back for the harbour. As the foremast

was being lowered, a large wave broke into the boat, washing the entire crew overboard. They had no sooner got back aboard after she righted, than she capsized for a second time, and all the crew found themselves in the sea again. Only one man was lost, Henry Storey, who was alive when dragged up the beach but later died from shock. A previous Newquay lifeboat, the **Joshua II**, had also capsized in 1868 whilst on practice, and having failed to right itself, caused a serious lack of confidence amongst her crew until replaced.

Over the next 18 years the **James Stevens No.5** was launched 18 times on service but came to an unfortunate end in December 1917. She put out in a NE gale to the SS **Osten,** of Copenhagen, which had lost her funnel and half her superstructure in bad weather and was at the mercy of the sea, drifting helpless towards the coast. Only yards out from the lifeboat slip a huge wave threw the **James Stevens'** beam on to the breakers, a second pushed her sail flat into the sea, and initially she refused to right herself. Blown beneath the cliffs, her 13 crew were rescued by ropes thrown from the shore, Bowman Clemens being the only minor casualty. Damaged beyond repair, the lifeboat slowly broke up, and was thought to have gone completely to pieces until 2004, when four Newquay sport divers found her lower hull section still intact amongst the rocks. By coincidence, Gareth Horner, one of the divers, is the grandson of the boat's original 2nd coxswain, Richard Trebilcock, who was awarded a Bronze Medal by the RNLI for the attempted rescue, Coxswain Gill receiving a Silver Medal.

St Ives – 1938

The first lifeboat at St Ives was named *Hope*, a locally built boat 30ft long, rowing eight oars, stationed there from 1840. A total of six other lifeboats served at that station up until 1938 when, following two disastrous accidents the station was temporarily closed. During the intervening years, the six boats between them saved a remarkable 416 lives, but in less than twelve months the station lost two lifeboats with the death of seven crew, plus 37 seamen from the two shipwrecks involved. The first of these two losses was the *Caroline Parsons*, the first motorized lifeboat stationed at St Ives. She entered service in 1933, having been built by White & Co at Cowes, Isle of Wight, paid for by the legacy of a Miss Caroline Parsons, of Edinburgh. Prior to being lost, she had launched on four service missions, saving 55 lives, and was bringing an additional 23 wreck survivors to shore when she met with disaster.

Just after 7pm on 31 January 1938, during a severe storm, the 3,700-ton SS *Alba* of Panama from Barry Docks to Civita Vecchia, with coal, sought the shelter of St Ives Bay, but ran ashore on the north-west side of St Ives Island. The lifeboat was launched into heavy seas, and anchoring near the wreck, veered down on the casualty. Unfortunately, her anchor failed to hold and dragging in a fast ebb tide, Coxswain Cocking ordered the *Alba's* crew to get aboard immediately, but it was some seven minutes before the men appeared, each carrying their belongings in suitcases! It is not recorded what the coxswain said to them, but certainly none of the luggage made it onto the *Caroline Parsons*. Overloaded with 23 survivors and nine crew, the lifeboat pulled away from the ship, going astern on her engine. The survivors were told to lie down on the deck to lower the boats centre of gravity, but as she cleared the bow of the wreck, a tremendous wave struck her beam on and she capsized, throwing nearly everyone into the sea.

The wreck and lifeboat were both so close inshore they were easily illuminated by car headlights, searchlights provided by the LSA (Life Saving Apparatus) crew and even torches held by wives and other relatives of the St Ives' men. An anguished cry went up from hundreds of spectators as the boat was seen to capsize, which self-righted itself in a matter of only seconds. The coxswain was saved by his son, who pulled him back into the cockpit, and then between them they got the entire lifeboat crew back on board, remaining with the boat till she crashed onto the rocks. A rocket line was fired across the lifeboat by the coast-guard LSA team, by which means the men were rescued, bystanders plunging into the surf waist-deep to lend a hand and get them to safety. None of the lifeboat crew was lost, although some were badly bruised or injured, but of the 23 men from the wreck, five drowned, and the lifeboat was a total wreck.

The coxswain received the RNLI's Silver Medal and the Hungarian government's Gold Cross of Merit, whilst each of his eight crew received RNLI Bronze Medals, inscribed vellum certifi-cates and a monetary award. A second Hungarian Gold Cross was presented to the town's Mayor, in recognition of the courage of those locals who assisted in the rescue. Tragically, five of those men were to lose their lives in the second, far worse, St Ives lifeboat disaster, less than a year later. There is a record of a previous St Ives lifeboat, the **Moses**, having capsized twice on service on 28 October 1865, going out to the French brig **Providence**. On that occasion for saving four men in almost impossible conditions, Coxswain Levett was voted a Silver Medal, along with monetary awards to him and the crew, in addition to £115 raised by public subscription and shared between them. However, the greatest recognition came from Napoleon III, Emperor of France, who sent a Gold Medal for the coxswain and a Silver Medal to each crew member, the first award of its kind given to a British lifeboat crew.

St Ives – 1939

It was the coastguards who reported to the St Ives lifeboat secretary at 2am on 23 January 1939, that a vessel was in a dangerous position two miles NNE of Cape Cornwall, to the west of St Ives. Aware that the Sennen Cove lifeboat could not be launched due to the state of the tide, Coxswain Thomas Cocking spoke to the St Ives' Secretary by telephone, and ignoring the violent gale which was blowing ordered the assembly maroons to be fired. The loud double 'booms' echoing over the little harbour must have struck fear into the hearts of the wives and families of the lifeboat crew, who knew the risk their menfolk would be taking going out in such a gale. Following the destruction of the **Caroline Parsons** the previous winter, the new Padstow lifeboat, the **John & Sarah Eliza Stych**, a slightly smaller replacement motorized boat, built by Saunders Roe on the Isle of Wight in 1931, had been allocated to the St Ives station, and it was this boat that put out that dreadful, fatal night.

Once clear of the shelter of St Ives Head, the lifeboat met the full force of the NW gale. About a mile and a half NNE of Clodgy Point she planed down a steep trough then sheered off, so that the next wave struck her starboard bow a terrific blow, and she went right over. Self-righting,

▲ *On 23 January 1939, the 'new' St Ives lifeboat* John & Sarah Eliza Stych, *put out to a vessel thought to be in distress in a terrible gale. After capsizing three times, only one lifeboatman was left alive, and after the boat was thrown up on the rocks at Godrevy, badly damaged, it was decided it should be burnt, to discourage souvenir hunters.*

(St Ives Museum)

as were all lifeboats by now, she came upright within seconds, but half of her eight man crew were missing, including her coxswain. A fifth member, Bowman William Freeman, was also thrown into the sea but was fortunately grabbed and pulled back aboard by two men. The engine stopped automatically on capsize, but then refused to re-start, offering no chance of picking up the missing men. Three times the engine fired, but immediately stalled, and the men had no choice but to anchor, then burn red and white flares calling for assistance.

When the anchor cable eventually parted, the boat could only drift to leeward, towards Godrevy Point. Ashore, all the help available was mustered; the St Ives and Portreath LSA crews making for Godrevy, whilst the Penlee lifeboat, stationed between Newlyn and Mousehole on the south coast, put to sea at 5am, and other lifeboat crews on the north coast were put on stand-by. On board the stricken lifeboat, the mechanic, Richard Stevens, must have cursed that engine, as time and time again it fired, started, and then stalled, presumably with something fouling the propeller. Two-thirds of the way across St Ives Bay, she was struck by another huge sea, capsized for a second time, and

on righting it was found the mechanic had disappeared overboard. Only three of the original eight crew now remained on board. As she approached the rocks of Godrevy Point, she capsized for a third time, and when she finally righted, William Freeman, the bowman, found he was the sole survivor. The sea threw the shattered lifeboat high up on the rocks, from where Freeman reached the cliffs which he managed to climb, then staggered to Godrevy Farm, where he managed to pass on the tragic details before collapsing.

News of the tragedy reached St Ives a little after 7am, plunging the entire community into grief and mourning. Many lifeboats have been lost elsewhere around the country, either with all hands or many of their crew, but this was no consolation to such a small tight-knit community where everyone knew each other. Several of the drowned men were related, the two Barbers being brothers, and young Cocking was the son of the coxswain, Thomas Cocking, who had devoted over 43 years to the lifeboat service. Each of the seven men was posthumously awarded the RNLI Bronze Medal, including the sole survivor. The irony of that dreadful night was that the identity of the vessel to which the lifeboat had put out was never known for certain. A steamship, the 3,000-ton *Wilston,* was found wrecked next day at Tregerthen Point, towards Land's End, and it is possible she was the vessel in question. Carrying a crew of 32, she was lost with all hands. Following this second tragedy, the St Ives lifeboat station was closed and only re-opened on a supposedly temporary war basis in 1940, but in fact remains open to this day.

Cornwall's most famous 19th century rescue

The long list of RNLI awards for rescues by Cornwall and Isles of Scilly lifeboats make it immediately apparent that of the five Gold Medals, 129 Silver and 61 Bronze presented since 1824, the majority went to St Ives and Padstow men, followed by Sennen, St Mary's (Isles of Scilly), Penzance and Penlee in that order. Whilst every lifeboat station, their crews, secretaries, helpers and supporters, are equally dedicated to this unique voluntary service, of the 25 stations historically sited in the Duchy, four of them, St Agnes, Hayle, Mullion and Portloe, have been unfortunate in never having received a single gallantry medal between them.

The introduction of RNLI medals for meritorious service saw some stations receiving exceptionally large numbers of awards for rescues, the Ramsgate lifeboat *Bradford* and its escort tug *Vulcan*, being a prime example. In January 1881, attending the famous wreck of the barque *Indian Chief* in the mouth of the Thames, a service lasting 26 hours, Coxswain Fish received a Gold Medal, and the two crews 18 Silver Medals. The Holyhead lifeboat earned one Gold and 10 Silver in February 1908, followed by perhaps the most famous of all Cornish rescues, involving the Whitby snow *New Commercial*, in January 1851. She struck at night, in fog and a full gale, on a ledge connecting the Great and Little Brisons, two huge rock outcrops a mile SW of Cape Cornwall, Land's End, so that no one saw the vessel go to pieces, leaving nine crew and the captain's wife clinging to a ledge. A sharp-eyed Cape Cornwall coastguard scanning the Brisons next morning with a aid of a telescope sighted the survivors, but at 9am a wave swept the ledge, drowning seven men, leaving only Captain and Mrs Sanderson, and one sailor. The latter, a mulatto named Isaac Williams, using his initiative, created a craft of sorts from a spar and rigging, and with a plank as a paddle and a scrap of canvas for a sail, got into Whitesands Bay, where he was picked up by fishermen. The Revenue cutter *Sylvia* was ordered round from Penzance, whilst the area coastguards assembled at Cape Cornwall, overlooking the Brisons. A boat from the *Sylvia* attempted to reach the rocks, but failed due to heavy seas, and repeated rescue attempts went on all day in atrocious conditions until nightfall. By dawn next day six rescue craft were in the area, watched eagerly by cliff top spectators estimated to be 5-6,000.

The second of two 9-pounder Dennett line-rockets fired from a boat fell across the ledge on which the two pitiful figures crouched. Mrs. Sanderson, a non-swimmer, wearing nothing more than a thin nightdress, tied the line round her waist and urged on by her husband, leapt reluctantly into the sea. At that moment three huge waves broke clean over the Brisons, the spray blotting out all sight of the boats and rescue from Cape Cornwall for several minutes, and the crowd thought the worst. The poor woman was pulled from the sea into a rescue boat, but exhausted and suffering dreadfully from cold and exposure, she died before they could get her ashore. The captain was saved by the same means, his drowned crew and wife later being interred in Sennen churchyard. For such a dramatic and difficult rescue lasting two whole days, conducted under the critical eyes of almost everyone living in the the Sennen area, Captain Davis was promoted to become the RNLI's inspector of lifeboats and awarded a Gold Medal, the captain of the cutter also received a Gold Medal, with Silver to 11 other men, and financial awards to two local miners and eight fishermen who manned the various rescue boats.

An early Isles of Scilly rescue

The embryonic *Royal National Institution for the Preservation of Life from Shipwreck* received in 1837, a donation of £26.19s.6d (£26.97p), collected by the people of the Isles of Scilly through Captain Charles Steel RN the islands' inspecting commander of coastguard, towards the cost of a lifeboat. Whilst this may appear a meagre sum, it was in fact a quarter of the cost of a new boat and it must be remembered the extreme poverty of the islands at that time. The management committee agreed to transfer the former 20.5ft Brighton lifeboat, built in 1824 by William Plenty, to the islands, which arrived at St Mary's that September. A boathouse was built for her on the Thoroughfare, in the middle of Hugh Town, but considered too small and unsuitable for Atlantic sea conditions she was condemned and broken up, unused in the two years she had been on Scilly. It was replaced in 1840 by another second-hand lifeboat of 26.5ft, rowing ten oars instead of only six, previously stationed at Plymouth. Her one and only service launch was in January 1841 to the Dublin steam packet *Thames*, a paddle-steamer en route to London with a crew of 26, a general cargo, 23 army recruits and soldiers, and 12 passengers. Captain Grey mistook St Agnes light for the Longships, passed through the North Channel and drove ashore close to Jacky's Rock, between Rosevear island and Crebawethan Neck at 5am, during a westerly gale accompanied by heavy snow. The six-oared pilot gig *Whale*, belonging to Mr Stidiford, a St Mary's shipbuilder, was the only boat able to reach the wreck and saved three women. The lifeboat was eventually launched, Scillonian men proving reluctant to man her, and it was no coincidence that the four Silver Medals later awarded by the Institution went to the first four volunteers. The lifeboat got no further than St Agnes where it was forced to shelter, its only part in the rescue being the recovery of eight bodies. Captain Steel, the coastguard officer, who acted as coxswain when no one else would take the responsibility, deservedly received the Institution's Gold Medal. That lifeboat was never used again and in 1855 the St Mary's station was closed and not re-opened for 19 years, despite being the only one in an area notorious for shipwrecks.

Padstow women to the rescue

Whilst the Grace Darling rescue of 1838 in the Farne Islands, for which she and her father received Silver Medals is enshrined in folklore, less well known is the award of Silver Medals to five Padstow girls in 1879. Four spirited sisters of the local Prideaux-Brune manor house family had been joined by Nora O'Shaughnessy, a friend, for an afternoon's rowing in the Camel estuary in very rough conditions on 9 August. They witnessed a boat capsize off Bray Hill, and rowing through heavy seas which entailed crossing part of the Doom Bar, not only saved the life of a drowning sailor but managed to get him into their boat and land him back at Padstow harbour. The sisters, Ellen, Gertrude, Mary and Beatrice, and their Padstow companion Nora, all received Silver Medals for their spirited rescue in extremely difficult conditions.

▲ *The four sisters, Ellen, Gertrude, Mary and Beatrice Prideaux-Brune, of Padstow,*
with a friend, Miss Nora O'Shaughnessy, who saved a drowning sailor from a
capsized boat off Bray Hill, Padstow, on 2 October 1879. Out for a quiet afternoon
row on the Camel Estuary, the five girls were being towed back to harbour by a
fishing boat, when they witnessed a craft go down. They asked to be cast off, and
rowed through very heavy seas generated by a sudden squall to a man's rescue,
getting him aboard only after a considerable struggle. All five girls received a RNLI
Silver Medal for their bravery and initiative.

(The Story of the Sea, *by Sir Arthur Quiller-Couch, 1895)*

Four lifeboats save 456 people from the *Suevic*

On 17 March 1907 the White Star liner SS **Suevic**, Australia to Liverpool with 524 passengers and crew, went ashore in fog on Maenheere Rocks off the Lizard. Both the Lizard and Cadgwith lifeboats launched, and escorted two ship's boats, full of women and children, to shore. When it was realized how many people were still on board, both the Coverack and Porthleven lifeboats were summoned to assist, and by noon the following day, the 18th, everyone had been saved without a single casualty, a most remarkable effort, especially with 60 children on board under the age of three. The Cadgwith crew saved 227 people, the Lizard 167, Coverack 44 and Porthleven 18, a further 68 being rescued by Falmouth tugs. The secretary of the Cadgwith lifeboat and its coxswain both received a Silver Medal, as did the first and second coxswains of the

▲ *Following the rescue of all 524 passengers and crew aboard the liner Suevic, in March 1907, by four Cornish lifeboats from the Lizard, Cadgwith, Coverack and Porthleven, the wreck was cut in two by salvors using explosives. The stern section, which still contained her boiler and engine rooms, was towed to Southampton where a new bow section was fabricated and attached, allowing her to return to service.*

(Richards Studio)

▲ *The* Ann Newborn, *Sennen 1919 - manned ready for a practice launch on the rough caunse slipway. (Tony Pawlyn)*

Lizard boat, as well as two seamen from the wreck who had carried on their backs numerous children down rope ladders from the wreck into the lifeboats.

Fourteen medals for a rescue by the Sennen Cove Lifeboat

On passage from Queenstown, three Royal Navy Armed Motor Launches were under escort of a destroyer to Southampton when HM ML **No. 378** took a heavy sea off Land's End on 30 November 1919, which disabled her engine. Twice towing hawsers were passed across from the other motor launches, but both parted,

leaving **No. 378** drifting helpless towards the Longships Rocks, which were buried in white water.

The Sennen Cove lifeboat, **Ann Newbon,** a pulling and sailing boat with a crew of 14, which had been on station since 1893, put out to assist and reached the tiny warship in time to see her nine crew abandon ship in a wooden dinghy which immediately capsized, throwing them into a boiling sea only a short distance from the reef. Four of them managed to get back aboard the launch just as it was thrown onto the rocks, where they scrambled ashore. Meanwhile the lifeboat continued to circle in the breakers, and it should be remembered that it was powered only by men pulling on ten oars. They succeeded in picking up four of the five crew still in the sea, and then Coxswain Thomas Nicholas turned his attention to the men stranded on the rocks, which were frequently buried in breaking seas. Four times the lifeboat was veered down to the reef on her anchor line, and on each occasion a man was plucked to safety until all four were safe, a rescue which required outstanding seamanship, courage, and determination in the most appalling conditions imaginable. No wonder the RNLI saw fit to present both the first and second coxswains with a Silver Medal, and a Bronze Medal to every other member of their crew. The latter award was still relatively new, having only been introduced in January 1917.

The crews of St Mary's lifeboat and three local boats earn 43 medals

It was the sound of a ship's siren from the direction of Scilly Rock, west of Bryher, Isles of Scilly, on 27 October 1927, that caused the open boat *Czar*, and motor boats *Ivy* and *Sunbeam* to put to sea that foggy, rough afternoon. They found the 6,892-ton Italian owned SS *Isabo*, laden with grain,

ashore in a heavy ground sea, with a strong gale developing. The 30ft *Czar* managed to pick up 19 survivors, the larger *Ivy* just one, which then took on board 11 men from the overloaded *Czar* and returned to Bryher. When the *Sunbeam* appeared towing a dinghy, this was used to take three men off the wreck and later a further eight. It was late afternoon when the lifeboat *Elsie* reached the scene, and Coxswain Lethbridge found conditions so treacherous, that he was forced to take the lifeboat into the shelter of New Grimsby harbour for the night, despite leaving four men clinging to the rigging on the *Isabo*. At first light the local doctor, William Ivers joined the lifeboat, and she returned to the scene of the wreck, but despite firing three rocket lines, the Italians seemed not to know what to do with them. Eventually the sea washed the men out of the rigging and they were picked up out of the sea. At the last moment another survivor was seen on Scilly Rock, and he too was rescued. Of the 38 crew, 28 were saved. Coxswain Lethbridge (Snr) and Charles Jenkins of the *Sunbeam*, both received RNLI Silver Medals as well as Silver Medals from the Italian government for outstanding service. The doctor, lifeboat mechanic and three other local boatmen received Bronze Medals from the

RNLI, and between the rescuers, 21 vellum certificates for bravery and a further 34 Bronze Medals were presented by the grateful Italians, for a rescue that is still considered as meritorious as any in the history of the islands.

The *Flying Enterprise* rescue and her secret cargo

An American general cargo vessel of 6,711-tonnes gross, built by the Consolidated Steel Corporation in 1944, the steam turbine driven *Flying Enterprise* spent all six years of her short life employed in the Atlantic, missing the Pacific war against the Japanese completely. Owned by the US Isbrandtsen Corporation, she was on passage from Hamburg to Baltimore in late December 1951, when hurricane force winds of 70mph made Christmas one her crew and the rest of the world would never forget.

She was labouring heavily in cross seas some 380 miles W of Land's End, when a huge stress crack developed across her upper deck, and she took a 30° list to port as the sea flooded her forward holds. In response to her Mayday radio distress call, the USN transport vessel *General Greely* and the USS *Southland* went to her rescue, taking off ten passengers, which included women and children, as well as 35 crew, with

the exception of Captain Carlsen, who refused to leave his ship. After three days standing by the crippled freighter, the US Navy ship was running low on fuel, and was replaced by another transport vessel, the *Golden Eagle*, and later the destroyer USN *John W Weeks* was dispatched from Plymouth.

At this point questions were already being asked by the media, what was so special about the *Flying Enterprise* that gave cause for the United States Navy to offer all this support? At this point the 1,136-tonne salvage tug *Turmoil* entered the scene, which was to become almost as famous as the freighter itself. Caught up in the same hurricane was the cargo ship SS *Mactra*, and the tug having successfully got a wire aboard, was able to tow her to Falmouth docks. Having reached port safely, Captain Dan Parker refuelled his vessel, the crew enjoyed a night's sleep alongside, and within 24 hours the tug left on 2 January 1952 to assist the *Flying Enterprise*, which had drifted to within 100 miles of Falmouth. By now the wreck was lying over at an angle of 80°, but still Captain Henrik Kurt Carlsen, from Denmark, refused to abandon ship, and to the delight of the media was joined by the *Turmoil*'s 1st mate, Kenneth Dancy.

The first journalist on the scene was George Ellis, a very well known freelance photographer based in Cornwall. He was repeatedly 'warned off' by the commanders of the US support vessels.

Despite the acute angle of the ship's deck and the obvious danger the two men were in should she suddenly sink, they appeared totally unconcerned, and many aerial photographs were taken of the two men sitting together on the ship's starboard railing, enjoying a cigarette and a quiet joke. With **Turmoil** dragging the ship nearer to Falmouth at a desperately slow 3.5 knots, hopes were entertained she could be saved, but on 9 January, within 50 miles of the port the towing wire parted, and could not be reconnected. On the 10th, realising the fight was lost, Captain Carlsen and Dancy calmly walked the length of her funnel, dropped off onto the deck of the **Turmoil**, and at 4.12pm watched the **Flying Enterprise** turn over and sink in 280ft of water at 49 40°N, 04 15°W, landing on the seabed on her port side. Carlsen later

▲ *Beached deliberately in order to save the lives of her crew,*
people from Bude watch as local men wade out into the surf
in an attempt to rescue survivors from the St Ives registered
Giles Lang *8 November 1896.*

(Richard Larn Collection)

received Lloyd's Silver Medal for Meritorious Service in recognition of having stood by his ship.

During July and August 1953, the Italian salvage company Sorima moored over the wreck, and divers recovered some $60,000 in bank notes, but a further $100,000 could not be found, neither would the company disclose what else they recovered or for whom they were working, but it became patently obvious it was the US Government, which explained the UN Navy's earlier involvement. The sunken ship carried 1,270 tons of pig iron, 890 tons of African coffee, 55 tons of bone meal, 800 bales of peat moss, 65 bird cages, 5 tons of columbite ore, 260 tons of onions, and steel vans loaded with carpets, aluminium chloride, bagging and animal hair from India and a mysterious 71.8 tons of general cargo. Cargo does not get more general than carpets and onions, and the 'general cargo' on the inventory later turned out to be zirconium, which is used to encapsulate the fuel rods of nuclear reactors. In 1952 the process of refining zirconium from the metal hafnium was absolutely top secret, and refined zirconium was worth more than gold.

The secrecy and military importance of the *Flying Enterprise*'s cargo, the initial presence of US Navy ships, Carlsen's courage in remaining with his ship, and the subsequent employment of Sorima, explains everything, which the CIA and FBI continue to publicly deny. It is now known that the launch of the world's first nuclear submarine, the USS *Nautilus* was delayed by the sinking of the *Flying Enterprise*, which makes the story of this West Country shipwreck all the more interesting.

The tragedy of the *Union Star* and *Solomon Browne*

Cornwall had not suffered the loss of a lifeboat for 42 years until the Watson class Penlee lifeboat, the **Solomon Browne**, put out in

hurricane force wind conditions on 19 December 1981, and went down with all eight crew, as well as four survivors on board from the coaster MV **Union Star** she was attending. The coaster had suffered engine failure six miles east of the Wolf Rock, and drifted for miles before going ashore between Lamorna Cove and Porthcurno under steep cliffs. A salvage tug and a Royal Navy SAR helicopter were already in attendance when the lifeboat arrived on site, conditions being described as mountainous seas, a heavy ground swell, rain and poor visibility: in short, horrendous. Coxswain Trevelyan Richards made a series of passes alongside the coaster. At one stage the lifeboat was thrown onto the hatch covers of the ship. At the last moment when the coaster was almost ashore he managed to pluck four survivors from the coaster's decks, He then turned away and was going in to take off the remaining two survivors on the ship, two others having been washed overboard, when the lifeboat was thrown high into the air by a huge wave, to drop like a stone in the trough, presumably landing on top of a rock outcrop.

The loss of the lifeboat had a profound impact on the small community of Mousehole, and indeed all the nation, one of almost sheer disbelief, particularly coming so close to Christmas. A national appeal fund was set up and donations in the order of £3 million were collected for the widows, families and partners of the eight Penlee men who died. Coxswain Richards was awarded a posthumous RNLI Gold Medal, and the other members of the crew a Bronze Medal. They were well merited. Independent observers described the weather conditions as 'horrific' , with winds gusting over 100 mph, pitch darkness, heavy rain, and waves which defy the imagination, breaking close to shore at heights up to fifty feet. The

▲ *The capsized hull of the coaster MV* Union Star *lies on the rocks near Porthcurno 20 December 1981.*
(Richard Larn Collection)

Watson class was itself only 47' long. The helicoper crew made numerous attempts to lower a line to the **Union Star**, but were frustrated by the whipping of the mast, which once missed their main rotors by just three feet.

The tug was unable to follow the coaster into shallow water for fear of being wrecked itself, sea conditions made it impossible to pass a towing wire, and no one on the coaster could possibly have reached her bow to connect it anyway. Despite the efforts of the tug, the helicopter and the brave men from Penlee, the **Union Star** drove inexorably onto the rocks with the loss of all eight of its complement. Coxswain Richards refused to allow Nigel Brockman's son Neil to join him as one of the lifeboat's crew that night saying, 'No more than one from any family on a night like this'. Neil Brockman was later appointed coxswain of a replacement Penlee lifeboat.

Three other lifeboats, from Sennen Cove, the Lizard and the Isles of Scilly, all launched to search for the missing Penlee boat and survivors. The Sennen boat was forced to turn back in mountainous seas. The Lizard boat flogged its way west through 15 miles of 12m (40ft) head seas to reach the scene, while the St Mary's boat was driven 30 miles east, at one stage surfing a quarter mile on a single wave. Sixteen people lost their lives that night, but only eight bodies were ever recovered.

Maritime Life Saving Services Today

The lifeboat service generally has of course changed out of all recognition over the past 50 years. The lifeboats themselves are larger, more powerful, fully enclosed and better equipped to go long distances offshore, carrying equipment and electronics unheard of even a decade ago. Their crews go out on 'shouts' mostly strapped into shock absorbing seats, under cover and warm, protected against the elements by full immersion suits, safety helmets and inflatable lifejackets. Incidents on the coast or in shallow water may well be dealt with by one of the many new RNLI 'D' Class inshore inflatable lifeboats, and all types of craft can call on Search & Rescue helicopter support by the Royal Navy, Royal Air Force and Coastguard Services. These can all air-lift casualties to hospital, straight from the sea or the deck of a boat or ship, saving vital time and many lives as a direct result. SAR helicopters frequently fly in pairs, supporting each other as much as 300 miles offshore to pick up injured men from fishing

▲ *The Pendeen Watch LSA crew and bystanders assist in establishing a hawser connection with the motor coaster* Alacrity, *after she ran aground in Portheras Cove in fog, half a mile from Pendeen, on Friday 13 September 1963.*

(Clive Carter)

craft, or survivors from yachts or larger vessels in distress. Such rescues far out to sea are usually backed up by long-range Nimrod Coastal Command aircraft of the Royal Air force, which can drop life rafts and emergency supplies to survivors, offering a reassuring presence as they circle the area until helicopters or a lifeboat arrive. Such rescues are co-ordinated by one of 19 shore based coastguard MRCC (Maritime Rescue Co-ordination Centres and Sub-Centres) around the UK, which maintain a constant listening watch on the radio distress frequencies, directing resources and back-up to incidents as required.

Additionally, the Coastguard Service continues to operate cliff rescue teams, who regularly save the lives of people and animals stranded on beaches, in remote coves, or who have fallen from cliff tops. Mention should also be made of the National Surf Life Saving and beach Life Guard organisations. With ever increasing numbers of the public using the sea and tidal waterways for leisure, countless lives are also saved every year by these dedicated people. The men and women of these combined rescue services are deserving of praise for their courage and dedication in saving the lives of others, particularly the RNLI crews, who still reflect the same determined selfless spirit that lifeboat men have shown internationally, over almost three centuries.

A short bibliography of lifeboat history

Cockcroft, Barry (1995) *Fatal Call of the Running Tide* Hodder & Stoughton
Cox, Barry (1998) *Lifeboat Gallantry* Spink & Son
Dibdin, J & Ayling, J (1894) *The Book of the Lifeboat* Oliphant Anderson
Evans, Clayton (2003) *Rescue at Sea* Conway Maritime Press
Fry, Eric C (1975) *Lifeboat Design & Development* David & Charles
Kelly, Robert (1979) *For those in Peril* Shearwater Press
Leach, Nicholas (2000) *Cornwall's Lifeboat Heritage* Twelveheads Press
Morris, Jeff (1987-1992) *An Illustrated Guide to our Lifeboat Stations Parts 1-7* Coventry Lifeboats Enthusiasts' Society
Noall, C & Farr, G (1964–1968) *Wreck & Rescue* series Bradford Barton
Phillipson, David (1994) *All her Glories Past* Smith Settle Ltd
Sagar-Fenton Michael (2000) *Penlee, the Loss of a Lifeboat* Truran
Skidmore, Ian (1979) *Lifeboaat VC* David & Charles
Warner, Oliver (1974) *The Lifeboat Service* Cassell

▲ *The* Nefili *drove ashore in Dollar Cover, Land's End at 3am on 5 November 1972 and sat directly on top of a previous trawler wreck,* La Varenne. *The* Nefili *had lost her radar in a fire and went ashore in dense fog, her crew being saved by breeches-buoy from the cliff top.*

The smaller picture taken only a month later shows the power of the sea, the vessel having been literally torn to pieces. *(Richard Larn Collection)*

Acknowledgments

Richards, of Penzance (Morrab Library); RNAS Culdrose Photographic Section and PRO; Gibsons of Scilly; Illustrated London News; Royal National Lifeboat Institution, Poole; Clive Carter, Penzance; St Ives Museum; National Geographic; *The Story of the Sea,* Sir Arthur Quiller-Couch; John Behenna, Slapton, Devon; Tony Pawlyn; Ministry of Defence. *The Story of Padstow's Lifeboats,* Claude Berry